GAME-DAY YOUTH:
LEARNING BASKETBALL'S LINGO

Millions watch basketball games at gyms, arenas, or on TV. Others listen to games on the radio. Youths play the game in gyms and schoolyards, getting great exercise, working on their skills, and attending practices to learn more about a fantastic and fun team sport.

Whether you recently signed up for the basketball team, watch a brother or sister play, or want to learn more about this game, this book is for you.

Simple text, clear illustrations of the court and its markings, drawings of where the players play on the court, and pictures of the official's signals will help you know more about playing basketball, the players and positions, basic rules, and the meaning of basketball words.

Game on!

by Suzy Beamer Bohnert
Copyright © 2011
All Rights Reserved

Here's What Readers Are Saying About Game-Day Youth: Learning Basketball's Lingo

"Awesome!"
—Radio station WCUB, Manitowoc, Wisconsin

"Simply perfect for you and your kids!"
—Radio station WNMR, Burlington, Vermont

"Game-Day Youth: Learning Basketball's Lingo is a sequel to a prestigious Mom's Choice Award winner. The Mom's Choice Award honors excellence in family-friendly media, products, and services."
—Mom's Choice Awards®

Here's What Readers Are Saying About The Game-Day Youth Sports Series™

"Everything you need to know about baseball in one book."
—Radio station CKNX-AM 920, Wingham, Ontario, Canada

"The #1 sports series for youths and adults."
—NewsTalk radio 1490 WCHM, Clarkesville, Georgia

"A real hit with youths and their parents."
—Radio station CKOM-AM 1250, Saskatoon, Saskatchewan, Canada

"To speak the game, you need to know the language. "Game-Day Youth: Learning Baseball's Lingo" is a guide to understanding baseball and its many related aspects. Aimed at children who want to get more involved with the sport, "Game-Day Youth" is a fine gift to any aspiring young athlete."
—Midwest Book Review

"Game-Day Youth: Learning Baseball's Lingo is a recipient of the prestigious Mom's Choice Award. Parents and educators look for the Mom's Choice Awards seal in selecting quality materials and products for children and families. This book has been honored by this distinguished award."
—Mom's Choice Awards®

Here's What Readers Are Saying About The Game-Day Goddess Sports Series™

"A great read with terrific explanations for all the football terms."
– Philadelphia Eagles' Promotions Department

"We enjoyed the creative definitions. We use it as a reference source at women's events."
– Pittsburgh Steelers' Marketing/Community Relations Departments

"Having trouble keeping up with game-day banter? This is a lighthearted book and the resource you need. With humor and accuracy, Beamer Bohnert's glossary of handy phrases and terms is easy to use and places you among the informed."
– Virginia Tech Magazine

"I've been looking forever for a book like this!"
– Adamstown Area Library

"Many women will benefit from your book. Send my library a copy!"
– Everett Free Library

Here's What Readers Are Saying About The Game-Day Goddess Sports Series™

"Men, women, and children love this book because it's entertaining, funny, and informative. It's loaded with humor, easy to understand, and let's you learn about football painlessly."
—Culpeper Citizen

"The paperback tackles all aspects of the professional and college game humorously. A usable resource for anyone just learning the game."
—The Star News

"This book is the ultimate study guide for quickly learning the game of basketball. The history, descriptions, and definitions are concise and easy to remember. A must read for basketball novices who are eager to start talking hoops!"
—Eric Konkol, George Mason University men's basketball coach, 2006 NCAA Final Four semifinalist

"A must-have book for those well-versed in basketball and for those starting to learn the game. Buy the book now, read it immediately, and astonish others with how much you know about basketball because of this book."
—Hammond Basketball Camp

"Terrific humor, accurate information, and wonderful presentation. This book should be the only one on your reading list for basketball."
—Lackner Basketball Camp

Also by Suzy Beamer Bohnert

Binkie Learns to Fly
Game-Day Goddess: Learning Baseball's Lingo
Game-Day Goddess: Learning Basketball's Lingo
Game-Day Goddess: Learning Football's Lingo
Game-Day Youth: Learning Baseball's Lingo

Next in the Game-Day Youth Sports Series:™
Game-Day Youth: Learning Football's Lingo

Copyright © 2011 by Suzy Beamer Bohnert

All rights reserved. No part of this book shall be reproduced or transmitted in any form or by any means, including electronic, mechanical, or magnetic reproduction, or photocopying, without prior written permission from the publisher. No patent liability is assumed with respect to the use of the information contained herein. Although every precaution has been taken in the preparation of this book, the publisher and author assume no responsibility for errors or omissions. Neither is any liability assumed for damages resulting from the use of the information contained herein.

ISBN 978-1-4507-6055-3

Library of Congress Control Number: 2011901995
Library of Congress subject headings:
Basketball
Basketball — Dictionaries
Basketball — Juvenile Literature
Basketball — Terminology
Basketball — United States — Dictionaries, Juvenile
Basketball for children
Sports — Dictionaries

Cover designed by David Wu

Published by B&B Publishing

B&B Publishing
Visit our Web site and Author Online at
http://mysite.verizon.net/vzeug7mn/
bandbpublishing@hotmail.com

Printed in the United States of America

TABLE OF CONTENTS

Dedication	ii
Preface	iii
Overview	1
Basketball's Start	1
Playing Basketball	1
The Basketball Court and Equipment	1
The Players and Their Positions	2
Officials	3
Basic Rules and Playing the Game	3
Offense	7
Defense	8
Basketball Skills	8
The National Basketball Association	11
Diagram of The Court	13
Diagrams of Player Positions — Offense	14
Diagrams of Player Positions — Defense	14
The Player Positions	15
Diagram of Official's Signals	17
Definitions	18
Index	79

DEDICATION

To my kids, the greatest people in the world.

PREFACE

Having a son and daughter who love team sports makes it difficult to sit on the sidelines. My husband and I value the exercise involved in team sports, and we advocate for fitness in general.

While we continue to help our budding athletes work on their skills, attend practices, help coach teams, and cheer them on at games, we thought there was a need for a book for youths who enjoy basketball and want to learn more.

Our goal is to get youths involved in these sports — as well as you!

Many thanks to David Wu for his artistic renderings, which grace this book's front and back covers.

A final thank you to the National Federation of State High School Associations (NFHS), National Basketball Association, and the National Collegiate Athletic Association, which provided information and resources for this book.

OVERVIEW

Because of the sport's popularity, you undoubtedly will watch or play a basketball game, so it's important to know what's going on to enjoy the game. This section of the book will explain how athletes play basketball, outlining the basic rules in both professional and college games. It will tell you about basketball's start, the court and equipment, the players and positions, and the National Basketball Association. You'll see diagrams of the court, where the players stand, and the official's signals.

Basketball's Start

When basketball inventor James Naismith first knocked out the bottom of two peach baskets and hung them on walls at either end of a gym in 1891, he couldn't have imagined that basketball would grow to be one of the world's most popular sports, played by men, women, and children.

Playing Basketball

As the most popular indoor sport in the world, basketball is an exciting game with fast-paced play. It blends teamwork with player skills. If we start with the basics, two teams play against each other, and each team on the court consists of five players. The team with the ball is on offense and tries to make points. The team that doesn't have the ball is on defense and tries to stop the other squad from scoring. The squad with the most points wins the game. It is a hard game, considering that the basket is ten-feet high.

The Basketball Court and Equipment

Where do you play basketball? The game of basketball takes place typically inside on a rectangular, hardwood floor. Full-size courts are 94 feet long and 50 feet wide, while those courts used in high school are usually 84 feet long. To mark the court, there are sidelines denoting the length and baselines showing the width. A midcourt line divides the court in half and runs parallel to the end lines. Lines mark the free-throw lanes, free-throw circle, and center circle.

At the end of the court on each side is a basket and backboard. The basket is attached to the backboard above the floor. The basket has a rim, net, and support for the backboard. The rim is 18 inches wide and is bolted to the backboard 10 feet above the floor. Backboards for high-school teams are fan-shaped or rectangular, while college and pro teams use rectangular backboards. A net attached to the rim allows the ball to go through.

A basketball is round and colored brown or orange. It is about 30 inches in circumference, weighing between 20 and 22 ounces for games played by boys or men. For girls and women, they use a ball about 29 inches in circumference, weighing between 18 and 20 ounces. Basketballs are typically made of leather or rubber.

Players wear a uniform with a sleeveless shirt, socks, shorts, and tennis shoes with rubber soles. Shirts have a number on the back to let fans and officials know who the players are.

The Players and Their Positions

On one team there is usually a center, two forwards, and two guards. The players can go anywhere on the court, and each of these players must play on offense and defense, often doing different jobs. Because of this, teams change positions throughout the game, and may use, for instance, two forwards and three guards.

The guards are usually good dribblers, shooters, and passers. They play farther away from the basket than the center or forwards and are typically smaller and quicker than those players. The guards set up plays and lead the offense. A point guard may handle the ball a lot for his team and the shooting guard is an accurate shooter for his team.

Forwards roam in the space from the free-throw line to the baseline. Their strengths are rebounding and making shots from up close. Because of this, they are usually stronger and taller than the guards.

A squad's tallest player takes on the role of center. He scores baskets, grabs the ball when his teammates miss a shot, and does his best to block shots that the other team takes.

Substitute players help their teammates by coming into the game to rest some players and when their unique skills, such as shooting or defensive play, are needed.

Officials

At a basketball game, there are people that enforce the game's rules called officials. For a game, there is a referee, one or two umpires, one or two timekeepers, and one or two scorekeepers. Referees and umpires make sure the rules are followed, and they may both call fouls and violations. The person in charge of the game is the referee.

As for where they watch the game, an official will stay close to the offensive team's basket and the other stands close to the division line. When play switches to the opposite end of the court, the officials swap duties. When there's a second umpire, he stays near a sideline. When an official spots a foul or violation, he blows the whistle to stop play and the clock. The official then describes the violation or foul and uses a hand or arm signal. Afterward, play starts again.

Together, the scorekeepers and timekeepers sit at a table on the sideline. One works the electronic scoreboard. The other writes down the field goals, fouls, timeouts, and free throws in the scorebook. A timekeeper also runs the game clock and another timekeeper runs the shot clock if a team must shoot within a certain time frame. The timekeeper shuts the clock off each time the umpire or referee blows the whistle.

Basic Rules and Playing the Game

So what do the players do in a game? When a team gets the ball, the offense tries to take the ball to the frontcourt by passing and dribbling it among teammates. They are trying to maneuver into position to shoot and make a basket and score points.

On the other hand, the defense wants to make sure the ball doesn't go in the basket, so it blocks shots, takes the ball away from the opponents, and guards all the players on the other team, so that those players don't get in good scoring position. The backcourt is where a team protects the basket and tries to halt the other team from scoring.

Each team tries to rebound, or get the ball after someone has tried to make a basket on a field-goal try or most free-throw attempts. The team that catches the rebound has the ball again on offense. Because many teams miss their shots, rebounding is important to control the ball and have chances to score.

So how does a team score? A team can make two points when the ball goes through the basket and net on one shot. This is known as a field goal. A team can also score two points on a rebound, which means it gets the ball after a shot that hits the backboard or the basket's rim. The team can then shoot it at the basket to try and have it go in and make two points.

When a team scores a basket, the other team gets to have the ball and pass it inbounds from the end line. The team that scored is now the defense.

Three points are awarded when a ball goes through the basket and net on one shot made from approximately 22 feet in the corner to 23 feet, nine inches on the pro level and 20 feet, nine inches at the college ranks. This is the three-point line.

Floor violations typically happen when the team on offense does something like have a player take more than two steps without dribbling the ball or dribbling the ball, stopping, and then dribbling again. For these violations, a team typically turns the ball over to the other team.

Floor violations are minor, and they typically involve a ball-handling mistake or a player's location on the court. Personal fouls are more serious and involve contact between players that helps one team over another. Typically, a player will hold, push, charge, slap, or trip an opponent, or bump the arm or body of an opponent while they are shooting. These fouls are tracked and recorded as team fouls. Technical fouls are the most severe and involve serious infractions.

For each intentional, or flagrant foul, such as trying to injure an opponent on purpose by kicking him, this results in two free throws for the fouled player at the high school, collegiate, and pro levels. In the pros, the fouled team gets to keep the ball, too.

Technical fouls are called for unsportsmanlike conduct or obvious bad behavior. High school and college rules give two free throws to the opposing squad. High-school teams that were fouled get possession of the ball as well. Technical fouls in the NBA result in a free-throw opportunity and a throw-in for the violated team.

In college and high school, five personal fouls result in a person leaving a game replaced by a substitute. In the NBA, six personal fouls result in an athlete's replacement.

It is the official's responsibility to stop play after a foul by blowing his whistle. Then, the game clock halts. The official signals to the crowd what the penalty is by using his hands to do a set array of signals.

An athlete taking a shot, who is fouled during the process, receives two free throws if they didn't make the shot, and one if they did. For college and pro players attempting a three-point shot who are fouled while shooting and miss, they get three free throws. If they make the three-point shot, they get one free throw. For a foul against a player on offense not shooting, the team gets to keep the ball.

These fouls are tracked and recorded as team fouls. Once a team makes a specific number of personal fouls during a half or quarter, the fouled squad gets to take one or two free throws following each foul for the remainder of the half or quarter. This is called a penalty situation.

For high-school play, once an opposing team makes five fouls in a half, the fouled player gets to take a free throw. If the athlete makes that free throw, he gets a second shot. When this happens, it is called a one-and-one.

College has the rule where the one-and-one starts with the seventh foul against the opposing team in one half. Following the 10th foul in the half by the other team, the fouled player receives two free throws.

In the pro game, once the other team has five fouls in a quarter, a fouled athlete gets two free throws.

When a player on offense has the ball and makes a foul, the other squad gets to have the ball. There is no team foul and no additional fouls are added to the penalty count. All other fouls, known as team fouls, count toward the penalty situation.

A player goes to the free-throw line when an opponent violates the rules by making a technical or personal foul. The player fouled steps to the foul line, 15 feet from the backboard in the pros and 15 feet in college, and shoots one or two times at the basket — based on the foul — without anyone trying to block the shot.

The players who are not shooting the free throw then line up on each side of the free-throw lane, or foul lane, to get the rebound, with the team that is not shooting gaining the two slots nearest the basket. The remaining slots are filled by athletes from each team who position themselves in alternating slots.

To summarize, the team that was violated gets to shoot free throws, it may have the chance to do a throw-in, or it may have a combination of free throws and a throw-in. If the offense commits the foul, the defense then gets to have the ball for a throw-in. When the defense commits a rule infraction, the offense gets to shoot free throws, it may have the chance to do a throw-in, or it may have a combination of free throws and a throw-in.

There are time restrictions in basketball. Teams may lose the ball to the other squad because they held on to the ball too long. When the ball goes out-of-bounds, a team has five seconds to put the ball in play. High school and college ball require that the ball cross the division line within 10 seconds of having the ball put in play. Pro teams are limited to eight seconds. If a player on offense is covered tightly by a defender, he violates a rule in high school and college if he dribbles or holds the ball for more than five seconds in the frontcourt.

Additionally, there are violations for not shooting the ball within 35 seconds for college ball and 24 seconds in the pro game. One last regulation prohibits a player on offense from standing in the free-throw lane of the frontcourt for more than three seconds.

The players don't have forever to win the game. In fact, pro games last 48 minutes and a college game is 40 minutes. Each of the playing segments in pro ball lasts 12 minutes and is known as a quarter, or period. The playing segments in college ball last 20 minutes each and are known as halves. Halftime, where the players get instruction in private from their coach, lasts 15 minutes. High-school games are played in four eight-minute quarters.

If the teams tie at the end of the game, they will play in what is known as overtime. Overtime lasts until someone wins, and the periods are five minutes each.

Basketball uses two different clocks, a game clock and a shot clock. The game clock counts down and tells the players and fans how much time remains for play in each period. A game clock tracks time as soon as someone touches the ball after it comes on the court from a throw-in, or after a jump ball or a final missed free throw.

The clock doesn't run when the ball is dead. The clock starts again when there's a free throw, jump ball, or throw-in.

Regarding timeouts in the pro game, each team gets seven timeouts. The pros get a 20-second timeout during each half. During a timeout, teams discuss strategy with the coach. There are three timeouts for each overtime period.

In men's college basketball during televised games, teams get three timeouts and three timeouts for TV commercials. In overtime, each team gets one timeout per period.

Timeouts can be made at all times. Times when a player can call a timeout include when a player has the ball, someone is injured, or when the ball is dead, or the officials have stopped play because of a mistake in the score. For those who don't keep track of the timeouts and call one by mistake, they get a technical foul against their team.

Substitutes can come into the game to replace a teammate. The substitute goes to the scorer's table, tells them his name and number, and whom he's replacing. He waits in the substitution box for a dead ball. Then, the official calls him into the game.

What does the beginning of the game look like? The official gets the teams ready for a jump ball, where he tosses the ball up at the center of the court and the opponents try to tap the ball from the center circle to a teammate, who will then bring the ball toward the other team's basket.

There are other occasions when jump balls may be used: when going into overtime; when a ball goes dead; when two opponents make personal fouls at the same time during a loose ball; when two opponents make technical fouls at the same time; and when an out-of-bounds ball is touched at the same time by players from both teams.

Offense

The offense wants to get a player open, so that he can make a good shot. To do that, the players move, pass the ball, and dribble to make an opportunity for someone to shoot.

One style of play on offense involves a lot of movement by the players and passes to teammates to get a good shot. A team may set a pick or screen, which means an offensive player uses his body to legally block a defensive player, allowing a player on offense to escape to take a clear shot. By using these picks and screens, a team can free a player to make a basket or cause the defender to make a foul.

A second style of play on offense is the fast break. When a team gets the ball on a rebound at its defensive basket, it goes on offense, getting the ball down the court quickly to stop the defense from setting up well and to have the offense score as fast as it can after it gets the ball.

Defense

To keep the other team from scoring, a team may use its defense in many ways. For instance, it may choose a man-to-man defense. In this defense, each person on the team is responsible for guarding a specific person playing offense. If a team has a particularly talented player on offense, the offense may double-team him, which means two players on offense may cover one player on defense.

A team may also use a zone defense. For this defense, each player defends a particular area of the court, guarding that area when an opponent comes there. These defenses are called "2-1-2," "1-3-1, "2-3," and "3-2." For example, a "2-1-2" zone defense has two defensive players located between the free-throw line and the midcourt, one near the free-throw line in the free-throw lane, and two players near the basket.

High school, college, and pro teams can use zone and man-to-man defenses in a game.

A team may also press, which means guarding the other squad man-to-man in the backcourt or having the defense guard the rivals man-to-man from one end of the court to the other. This defense allows a team to make another team play without mistakes on offense or chance turning over the ball.

Basketball Skills

Every sport requires certain basic skills, and basketball is no different. These fundamentals, or basics, help young players do well. Some things to concentrate on while practicing include footwork, dribbling, passing, shooting, and defense.

Footwork deals with quickly changing direction, using speed, stopping and starting quickly, and moving with the play of the game.

To do so, bend your knees, put your rear out, and lean forward with your shoulders. Take your arms and hold them out to your sides, opening your fingers.

If you have one foot just ahead of the other, you can push off the back foot to give you some speed and use that front foot to bring you to where you want to be. Use your back foot to pivot to move your body and the other foot in a circle to look for a teammate to throw the ball to.

Dribbling requires that you keep your head up to see open players you may pass to and that you dribble with one hand at a time, using both the right hand and the left hand.

To dribble, bend your knees a bit and lean forward. Keep your other hand in a position that shields the ball from your opponent. When a defender comes close, dribble low and protect the ball by using your body while you move with the ball.

Players pass the ball to move it down the court. Different passes are used for certain situations.

When you want to get rid of the ball quickly, you would try the chest pass. Holding the ball with both hands, the player brings it toward their chest, stepping forward and pushing the arms straight ahead with the ball, snapping their wrists to get the ball to their teammate.

For a situation where the defender has his hands in the air, try the bounce pass. Holding the ball waist high with two hands, step forward and straighten the arms, making the ball hit the floor and go into a teammate's hands.

A good pass to throw the ball high, so the defense can't get it, is the overhead pass. To do this, the player holds the ball over his head with both hands. He quickly lets go of it by whipping his hands forward.

A shovel pass may be used to connect with a teammate running nearby. This requires using an underhand motion to get a pass to a teammate.

An outlet pass may be used following a defensive rebound if a player gets the ball and throws it downcourt to a teammate going there for a fast break. To do so, put the ball behind your head with one hand. Step forward with the other foot to make the same motion as if you were throwing a baseball, which is another name for this pass — the baseball pass.

Making shots in basketball helps a team win games. A player should try to get into position to make the shot that feels comfortable to them, taking their time, focusing on the basket, and staying balanced.

There are different shots that you can take, one of which is the lay-up. To do this, you dribble the ball down the court toward the basket. As you near the basket, you push off the floor and go in the air with your left foot while approaching the basket from the right side. While in the air, take the ball and push it on to the backboard, so that it goes in the basket. When you approach the basket from the left side, you will push off the floor with your right foot, once again taking the ball and pushing it on to the backboard.

The dunk shot is best performed by tall players because it involves jumping high and taking the ball above the rim. The athlete then pushes the ball through the basket.

The hook shot is most effective when taken close to the basket. You will turn sideways to the basket and lift the arm farthest from the basket to bring the ball straight above your head. Flick your wrist when the ball gets to the highest point, launching the ball toward the basket.

For shots from a greater distance, we call these "outside" shots. The first outside shot is the set shot. Younger players may be more comfortable using the two-hand set shot, which has you grasp the ball with the hands on each side. With fingers open, knees bent, and feet apart, you lift the ball, supporting it in your hands. You drive your body up, pushing the ball toward the basket with a quick snap of the wrists. For older players, a one-hand set shot places the ball in one hand while the other hand rests against the side of the ball to protect it and guide the ball on its way to the basket.

Jump shots are also used from a greater distance. The athlete has knees bent and the ball positioned as in a one-hand set shot. The player jumps with both feet off the floor, letting the ball go with a quick snap of the wrists.

Playing good defense is hard, but is important to keep the other team from scoring. When you guard a player on the other squad, you will want to bend your knees and keep your feet apart with one foot forward. For instance, if you keep your right foot forward, bring your right arm up to the level of your opponent's head, and keep the fingers open. With your left arm, have it outstretched, keeping it between knee and waist. For the times when you are guarding someone who has the ball, you want to block a pass or stop a shot. The hand to the side stops a pass and the hand at head level blocks a shot or high pass. When the other player starts to dribble, move along with him by shuffling or sidestepping.

For a player that moves in scoring distance, move toward him to cover him tightly. If a player is out farther away from the basket where a shot is not practical, you may stay several feet from him. If you are guarding someone near the basket who is waiting for a pass, stay between him and the basket, standing just behind him and using one hand to bat down a ball that comes to him.

Look at your opponent's waist when guarding him to see which direction he may go. He may fake with his head or other parts of his body, but the waist often gives a good sign of what he will do. If possible, try to stay on your feet, raising both arms up in the air when the other player takes a shot.

The National Basketball Association

The National Basketball Association (NBA) is the league of professional men's players. With an Eastern Conference and a Western Conference, there are 30 teams and six divisions.

The Eastern Conference is divided into the Atlantic Division, the Central Division, and the Southeast Division. In the Western Conference, there is the Southwest Division, the Northwest Division, and the Pacific Division.

Those squads in the Atlantic Division are the following: Boston Celtics; New Jersey Nets; New York Knickerbockers; Philadelphia 76ers; and the Toronto Raptors.

To make up the Central Division, we have the Chicago Bulls; Cleveland Cavaliers; Detroit Pistons; Indiana Pacers; and the Milwaukee Bucks.

The Southeast Division consists of the Atlanta Hawks; Charlotte Bobcats; Miami Heat; Orlando Magic; and the Washington Wizards.

As we look at the Northwest Division, we have the Denver Nuggets; Minnesota Timberwolves; Oklahoma City Thunder; Portland Trailblazers; and the Utah Jazz.

The Pacific Division has the Golden State Warriors; Los Angeles Clippers; Los Angeles Lakers; Phoenix Suns; and the Sacramento Kings.

The Southwest Division consists of the Dallas Mavericks; Houston Rockets; Memphis Grizzlies; New Orleans Hornets; and the San Antonio Spurs.

NBA teams play 82 games each season, with eight teams from each conference able to participate in games following the regular season to see who makes it to the championship playoffs.

For playoffs, teams within the two conferences are pitted against each other, with winners advancing, and a final game, known as the NBA Finals, played between the Western Conference champion and the Eastern Conference champion. The winner of the NBA Finals is considered the best team in all of professional basketball.

Diagram of The Court, The Player Positions, Player Positions on Offense and Defense, and Official's Signals

In this section, we'll see pictures of what the court looks like with its markings, what each player does in each position, where the players play on offense and defense, and the signals the official uses to make calls during a game.

THE COURT

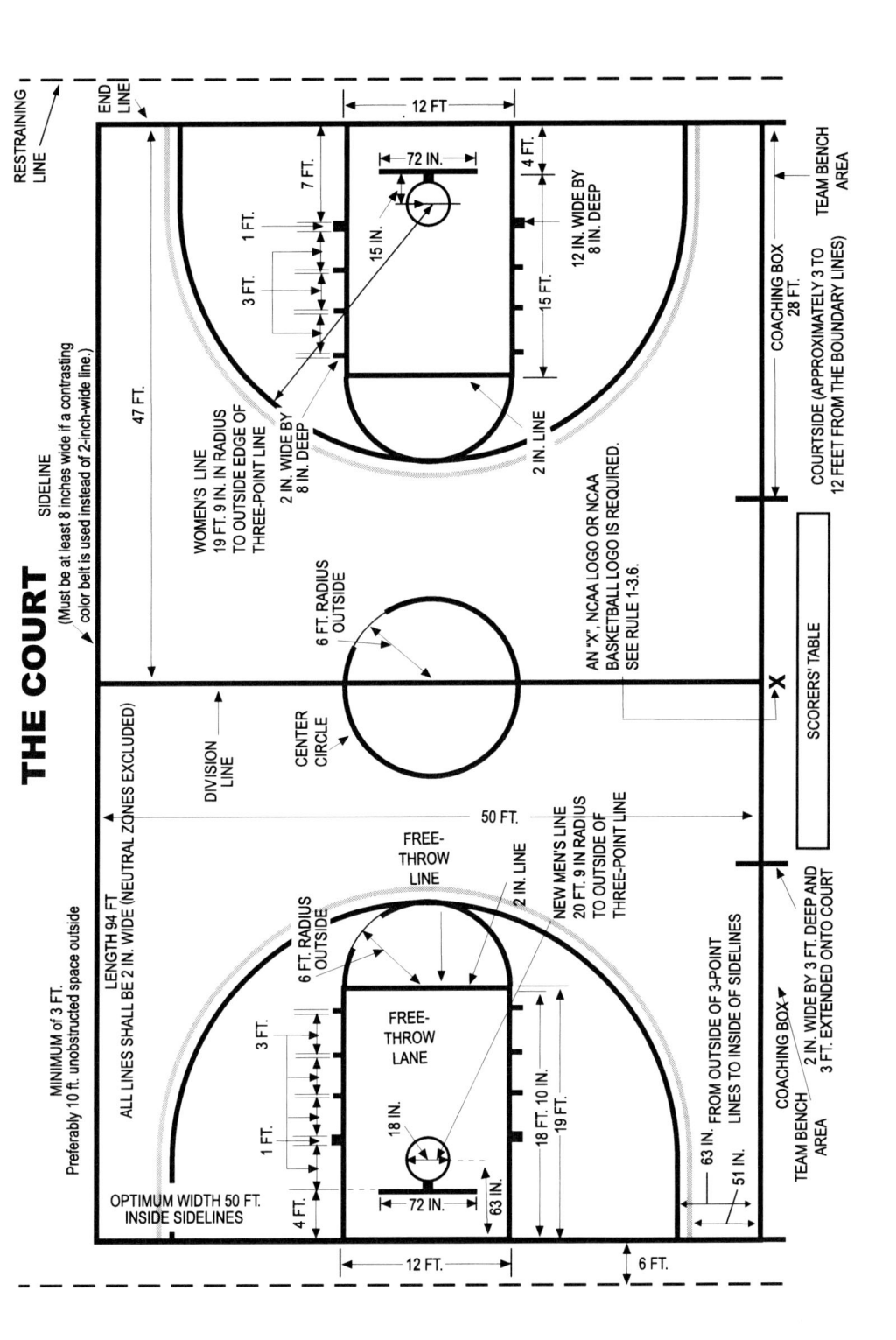

Player Positions — Offense

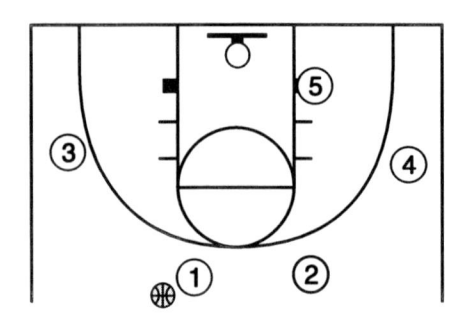

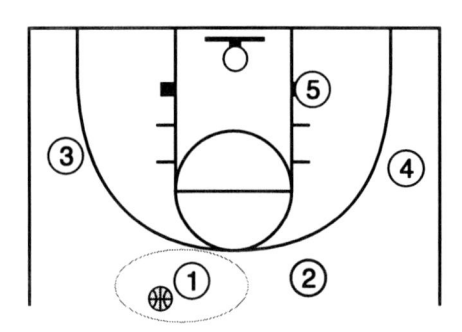

Offensive Players

① ② ③ ④ ⑤

Offensive players are represented by circles containing numbers corresponding to the basic five player positions.

1 = Point Guard
2 = Shooting or Off Guard
3 = Small Forward
4 = Power Forward
5 = Post or Center

Player with Ball

The symbol of a basketball indicates the player who starts out with ball possession.

Player Positions — Defense

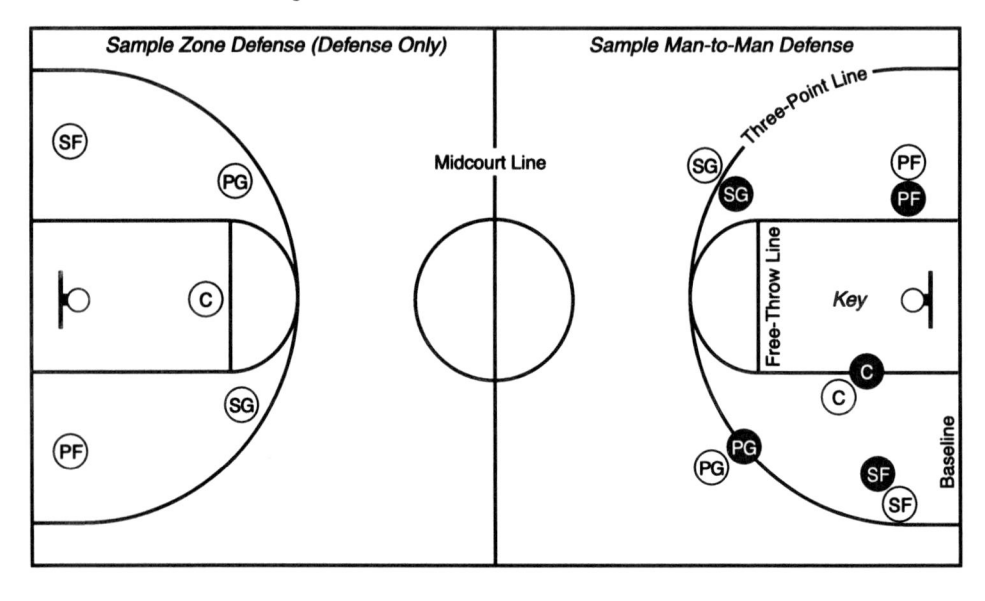

Sample Zone Defense (Defense Only)

Sample Man-to-Man Defense

Midcourt Line

The Player Positions

The abbreviations on the diagrams show where these players play when they are on defense and offense.

PG — Point guard
SG — Shooting guard
SF — Small forward
PF — Power forward
C — Center

On the court, five players from each team will play the main positions, which are the following: two guards, two forwards, and a center. Coaches typically assign a player to a position, but these roles do not have to be filled at all times. These are what the players do when they are on the court in one of these positions:

Point guards — These are good dribblers who are often asked to bring the ball up the court on offense while their teammates get set up in position. They can pass well to teammates who get open to score. They control the speed of play and call out plays. Usually they have a good jump shot and can drive in the lane to score points, too.

Shooting guard — Good shooters from long distances who are fast and able to dribble well. They can also steal the ball well on defense. They are the backup ball handler, and they get open and take a shot or pass the ball to a teammate who is open to make a basket.

Small forward — They shoot well from far away and can shoot close in, too. They are good rebounders, good passers, have speed, and can drive toward the basket.

Power forward — These players play near the painted area of the court and by the basket as they shoot from close range and do layups. On defense, they are important rebounders. These players try to get open for shots by using their strength.

Center—These players are tall and able to get rebounds and shoot from close range. On defense, they try to block the other team's shots and play in the painted portion of the court. They move around and get the ball to other players for shots, too, because of their strength, and they make contact with opponents during rebounding and on offense.

Official NFHS Basketball Signals

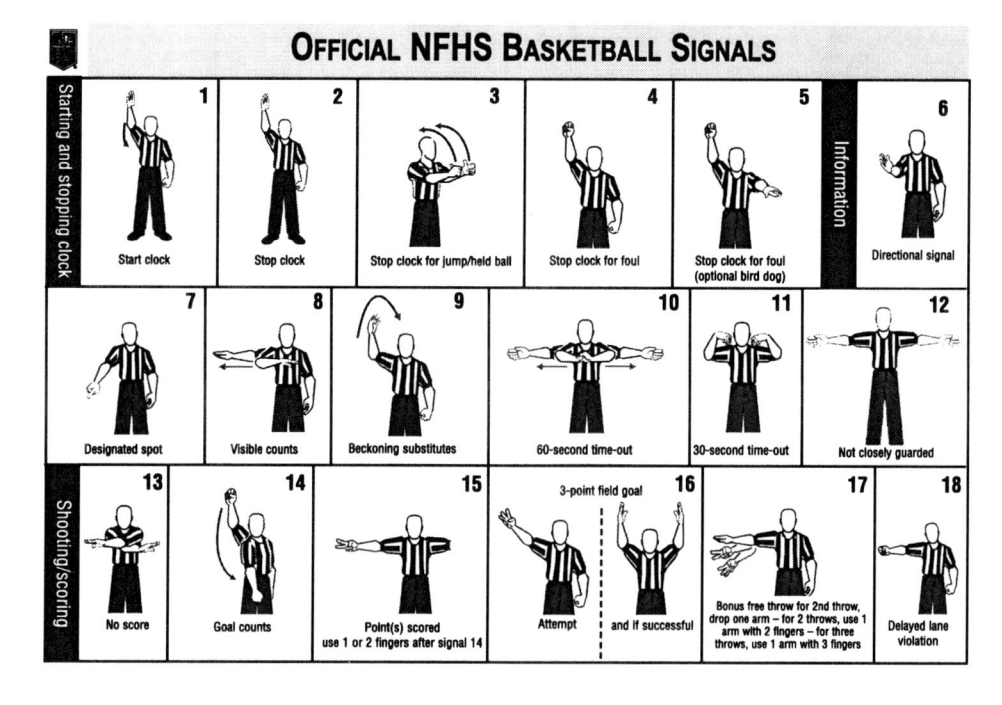

Starting and stopping clock

1. Start clock
2. Stop clock
3. Stop clock for jump/held ball
4. Stop clock for foul
5. Stop clock for foul (optional bird dog)

Information

6. Directional signal
7. Designated spot
8. Visible counts
9. Beckoning substitutes
10. 60-second time-out
11. 30-second time-out
12. Not closely guarded

Shooting/scoring

13. No score
14. Goal counts
15. Point(s) scored — use 1 or 2 fingers after signal 14
16. 3-point field goal — Attempt / and if successful
17. Bonus free throw for 2nd throw, drop one arm — for 2 throws, use 1 arm with 2 fingers – for three throws, use 1 arm with 3 fingers
18. Delayed lane violation

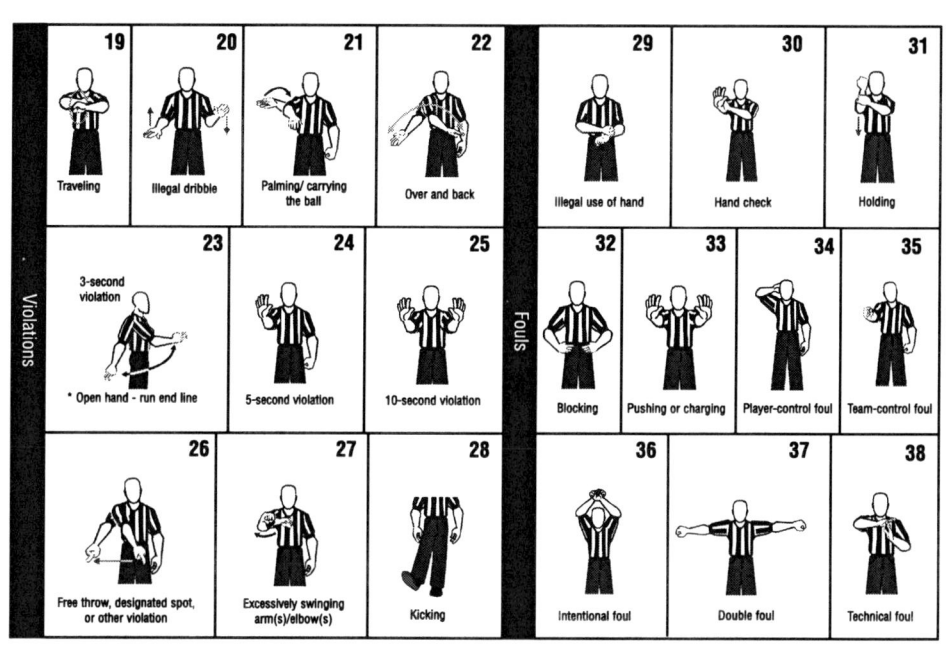

Violations

19. Traveling
20. Illegal dribble
21. Palming/carrying the ball
22. Over and back
23. 3-second violation — *Open hand - run end line
24. 5-second violation
25. 10-second violation
26. Free throw, designated spot, or other violation
27. Excessively swinging arm(s)/elbow(s)
28. Kicking

Fouls

29. Illegal use of hand
30. Hand check
31. Holding
32. Blocking
33. Pushing or charging
34. Player-control foul
35. Team-control foul
36. Intentional foul
37. Double foul
38. Technical foul

17

DEFINITIONS

Featuring all parts of the game, this portion of the book presents sports terms, explaining hard things in a simple way. Talking about words used to describe the offense and the defense, scoring, infractions, and signals, basketball followers will discover what they may have missed while playing, during game broadcasts, or afternoons in the stands.

Alphabetized for quick reference, many expressions common to college ball and the professional game appear.

Well, it's time to learn about definitions. Taking key words and phrases from the sports pages, television and radio broadcasts, and the courts where teams play everyday, we've put together a list of what you'll need to know to have the best basketball knowledge.

Italicized words appear as definitions on another page of the book.

A

air ball—A poor *shot* that misses the *basket* and *backboard*.

air dribble—This is a *traveling violation*. The other team gets to have the ball and throw it in from the *sideline*.

alive—The ball becomes alive and play starts when someone taps the ball during the *jump ball,* shoots it, or passes it *inbounds*.

All-America—This award goes out every year to the best college *basketball* players. They are picked for each of the positions on a team. Only the best players in the U.S. receive this honor.

All-Star—A pro *basketball* player chosen by fans. The player makes up a squad of the best players. He plays in the All-Star Game between the Eastern Conference and the Western Conference.

alley-oop shot—A shot traveling high in the air toward the *basket*. A pass sometimes thrown high in the air for another player to jump up and *tip-in* as he nears the *basket*.

alternating-possession rule—College rules say that after each *jump ball,* the *possession arrow* gives the ball to the other team. This allows for each squad to take turns having a *throw-in*.

assist—A pass to a teammate who *shoots* the ball right away without *dribbling* it or holding it.

The player looks to pass for an assist.

B

backboard — The backboard has the *basket* attached. Players use the backboard to try and *shoot* the ball off the backboard and into the *basket*.

backcourt — A team's area and *basket* that it defends. It is an area half the length of the *basketball* court and marked by the *center line*. This also means a team's *guards,* who bring the ball up the *court* on *offense*.

backcourt foul — A team *foul* that happens when a squad is on the same half of the *court* as its defensive *basket*.

backcourt violation — To avoid this *penalty*, players on *offense* must bring the ball over the *center line* within 10 seconds in college ball and eight seconds in pro ball. If they don't, they turn the ball over from the *sideline* at the point where the play stopped. Once a team goes past the *center line,* it must not throw or *dribble* the ball into the *backcourt*. If it does, it must give the ball to the other team to do a *throw-in*. This takes place from the *sideline* at the *center line*. See over and back.

backdoor — A player located underneath the *basket,* by the *end line.*

backdoor play — When a player on *offense* escapes the *defense*. He then goes to the *end line* and catches a *pass* from a teammate to make a *lay-up* while located underneath the *basket*.

ball boy, ball girl — These people are in charge of the team's basketballs and equipment each game.

ball control — Moving the ball around the court, keeping it under control. When an *offense* or *defense* doesn't want the other team to score, it will try to keep the ball by good *dribbling* and passing.

ball fake — A player on *offense* who pretends to *shoot* or *pass* the ball to a teammate, so he can get by the other team.

ball handler — The person with the ball or an athlete with a gift for passing and *dribbling*.

ball handling — This involves good passes and careful *dribbling* by the *offense* to get the ball up the *court*. With these skills, the *offense* can make some good *shots* to get *points*.

bang the boards, bang the glass — A player who moves with power to get near the *backboard* to grab *rebounds*. See *crash the boards, hammer the boards, pound the boards,* and *pound the glass*.

bank — Throwing the ball at the *backboard*.

bank shot — Throwing the ball at the *backboard,* hitting it, and hoping the ball goes in the *basket*.

barnburner — A game close in score.

baseball pass — A long, *overhead pass downcourt*.

baseline — This marks the end of each side of the *court*. This is a place where *shooters* try to make a *shot* right inside the *line*. See *end line*.

basket — Attached 10 feet above the floor, there is a basket at the end of each *court* where players try to make *shots*. If players make a basket with a *shot* from the *floor,* it's worth two or three *points,* based on the distance.

basketball — A game with teams of five players each. Each team tries to score more than the other squad by shooting at a *basket* and scoring. A leather ball.

Basketball Hall of Fame — Located in Springfield, Massachusetts, this museum features the finest *basketball* players. Named the Naismith Memorial Basketball Hall of Fame, it honors basketball's founder, Dr. James Naismith. See *Hall of Fame*.

basketball throw — Tossing a ball overhand.

basket interference — A *penalty* against a team for trying to stop a *shot* by touching it as it is about to go over the *rim*, or while the ball goes downward toward the *basket* before it hits the *rim*, or trying to touch it after it hits the *backboard*. For those who cause the *penalty*, the other team gets to throw the ball in from the *free-throw area*, or the *offense* gets two *points* — three *points* for the pros and some college teams — if the *shooter* was in the three-point range when the *penalty* happened. See *goaltending*.

beat the defender — This happens on *offense* when a player moves into place away from the defender, who should have guarded him.

bench — To take a player out of a game to rest him, because of *foul* trouble, or because of poor play.

big gun — Someone able to score many *points* for the other team.

big man — This refers to the *center*, because of his height.

blackout — When a game doesn't air on television because it's not approved.

bleachers — Indoor seats for fans.

blind pass — A difficult job that involves not looking at the person to whom you *pass* the ball.

blind side — The opposite side of where a player is looking.

block — On *defense*, to put the hands up to stop a *shot* from going in the *basket* or a *pass* from going to a teammate. This also means that a block can cause a *personal foul* if a player touches an opponent and gets in his path.

blocked shot — When a defender gets a hand or fingers on a ball that is going to the *basket* after a *shot* by a player on *offense*. This saves the *defense* from having a *basket* scored against it.

blocking — Getting in an opponent's way by pushing a hip, leg, hand, or body part in front of a moving competitor. This causes a *personal foul*.

block out — When a player gets in front of the opponent and tries to get the *rebound* or *tip-in* first. See *boxing out* and *screen out*.

blow — To make a needless mistake on an easy play. This also means when a team has a scoring *lead* and then loses it.

blow off the court — To beat another team by lots of *points*.

board — A *backboard* or a *rebound*.

bonus, bonus free throw — Once a team has a certain number of *team fouls* during a specific time, a player gets to *shoot* an extra *free throw* or two as an award. Pro ball awards the bonus free throw after five *fouls* during one *period*. In college, it's seven *fouls* during one *half*. The pros call a bonus free throw a penalty free throw.

bonus situation — Once a team has a certain number of *team fouls* during a certain time, a player gets to *shoot* an extra *free throw* as an award. The pros call this a *penalty situation* or *penalty stage*.

bounce pass — When an athlete passes the ball to a teammate by making it hit the floor to go in the teammate's hands.

box, box-and-one — A *defense* that puts two players on each side of the *free-throw lane*. These players play in a *zone defense*. The fifth defender plays man-to-man against the other team's high scorer.

boxing out — When a player gets in front of the opponent and tries to get the *rebound* or *tip-in* first. See *block out* and *screen out*.

box score — This appears in the newspaper or on the Internet. It lists each player's name, the game score, and individual game performance.

break—Also known as a *fast break*, this is when a player hustles down the *court*. This also means when a player goes in a different direction than thought.

bucket—Two *points*. This also means a *basket*.

buzzer—Signals the end of a *period* or game and makes a loud noise, so that everyone can hear it.

buzzer shot—An airborne ball going toward a *basket* as the *buzzer* sounds. The *buzzer* signals the end of a *period*.

bye—A team's step forward to the next tournament level without playing another team.

This player is making a bucket.

C

captain — The team leader and one who speaks for the team.

carry — When a player *dribbles* the ball and then picks up the ball in the palm of his hand. This is against the rules.

center — Plays against the other team's *center* in the *frontcourt*, close to the *basket*. Usually the team's tallest player, he helps *rebound, shoot, pass*, and handles the *tipoff*.

center circle — Where *jump balls* take place at the middle of the *court*. See *circle*.

center jump — When the *center* of each team goes to center court to jump for the ball at the start of the *period*.

center line — This line divides the *court* into the *backcourt* and *frontcourt*. It runs parallel to the *end lines*. See *division line* and *midcourt line*.

charge — A player on *offense* gets a *personal foul* if he runs into a defensive player set in his *position*. See *charging*.

charging — A player on *offense* gets a *personal foul* if he runs into a defensive player set in his *position*. See *charge*.

cheap shot — Hurting an opponent when he's caught off guard.

check — *Guarding* a player on the other team.

chest pass — Different from a *bounce pass*, this *pass* travels in the air as the *passer* pushes the ball out from his chest using two hands and outstretched arms.

choke — Not getting something important done because of nervousness.

circle — Where *jump balls* take place, at the middle of the *court*. See *center circle*.

clear the bench — When a team leads by a lot of points, the *coach* will put *substitutes* in the game, taking out the *first-string* players.

cliffhanger — A close game in doubt of a winner until the finish.

clinch — When a team wins a championship.

clock — Used by players and *coaches* to look at how much time remains in a game. The *shot clock* lets players see when they should take a *shot* before a squad gives the ball to the other team.

clutch shooter — An athlete able to shoot and score at important, close points in a game.

coach — To teach athletes a sport's basics and skills.

coast to coast — Includes the entire court's length, such as a *pass* from one end to the other.

cold — A period of time when a team doesn't score.

collapse — To stop a *center* from *passing* or *shooting* on *offense*, two or more defensive teammates will go toward the *center* when he has the ball in the *pivot*, or *frontcourt*, near the *basket* or outside the *lane*.

common foul — When this *foul* happens, the other team gets to throw the ball in from *out of bounds*. Known as a *personal foul*, it's not *flagrant* or *intentional*, or a *double* or *multiple foul*. When there is a *bonus situation*, a *bonus free throw* goes to the fouled player.

conversion — An athlete who makes a *free throw*.

convert — An athlete who *shoots* and makes a *free throw*.

cord — The *net*, attached to the basket's *rim*. See *net*.

corner — A spot where the *baseline* and *sideline* meet. There are four of these on a *basketball court*.

counterattack — When the team gets the ball and begins its offensive plan.

court — A hardwood *court* indoors for *regulation games*.

court vision — Seeing the whole *court* and where teammates and defenders are to send great passes to teammates.

cover — When a player *defends* against the other team or watches a part of the *court*.

crash the boards — A player who moves with power to get near the *backboard* to grab *rebounds*. See *bang the boards, bang the glass, hammer the boards, pound the boards,* and *pound the glass*.

crosscourt — The other side of the *court*.

crossover dribble — Taking the ball down the *court* by *dribbling* with the right hand, sending the ball to the left hand with a bounce, then *dribbling* the ball with the left hand, and sending it to the right hand with a bounce. The player repeats the motion down the *court*.

A player uses court vision to make good passes.

27

cut—Moving fast on *offense* to keep away from a defender while looking for a *pass* or getting in place to *shoot* a *basket*.

cylinder—A spot located above the *basket*. The *officials* watch for *goaltending* or *basket interference* here.

D

D — The *defense*.

dead ball — A ball *out of bounds* or ruled dead because of a *foul* or a rule *violation*.

default — When a team doesn't show for a game, allowing the other team a win.

defend — Trying to stop the other team from scoring.

defense — Not letting the other team *shoot* at the *basket*, score *points*, *dribble downcourt*, or successfully *pass* the ball.

defensive boards — Each team *defends* one side of the *court* and the *basket* on that side of the *court*. This is the *backboard* of that *basket*.

defensive rebound — The *rebound* that follows the missed *shot* by the other team.

diamond-and-one — Four men form a diamond on *defense* with one man on each side of the *free-throw line*, one man at the *high post* away from the *basket*, and one man at the *low post* near the *basket*. The last defender covers the other team's scoring threat.

disqualification — A player who goes out of the game because he has too many *fouls*.

division line — This line divides the *court* into the *backcourt* and *frontcourt*. It runs parallel to the *end lines*. See *center line* and *midcourt line*.

double-cover, double-team — To use two players at the same time on *defense* to *cover* one person on *offense*.

double dribble—Using two hands at the same time to *dribble* or stop *dribbling* the ball and then starting again. The other team gets to throw the ball in from *out of bounds* near where this *violation* happened.

double elimination tournament—Removing from a tournament a team that's lost two games in a row.

double figures—When a player has 10 or more *points, assists,* or *rebounds* in one game.

double foul—When two players on opposite teams *foul* each other at the same time. In college play, the ball goes to one team every other time if no one controlled the ball. If the *foul* happened when a team had the ball, then the ball goes to the place where play stopped and is awarded to the other team *out of bounds*.

double-pump—To lose a defender, a player on *offense* will pretend to *shoot* twice at the same time. This allows the offensive player to then *pass* the ball, *dribble,* or *shoot* again.

doubles—When someone scores, *rebounds,* or has *assists* in the double digits.

downcourt—The side of the *court* where a team *shoots* at the *basket*.

draft—Picking athletes to play for a pro team.

draw—A chance pick of competing teams fit for tournament play.

draw a foul—To move into place to receive an *intentional foul*.

draw sheet—A game-by-game list of participants in a tournament.

dribble, dribbling—To get down the *court*, a player pushes the ball to the *floor* with the fingertips of his hand, making it bounce. He stops the *dribbling* when he picks the ball up and holds it in his hands. A player must bounce the ball down the court and may not walk or run with it.

dribbler — An athlete with a talent for *dribbling*. This term also means a person with *possession* of the ball who is *dribbling*.

dribble series — How a player moves the ball down the *court*. He *dribbles* it until he picks up the ball in his hands.

drill — A practice for athletes letting them work on a part of the game, such as *dribbling*, passing, or shooting. This also means when a player throws the ball hard.

drive — Powerfully heading toward the *baseline* or *basket* with the ball to get it in the *basket*.

drive to the basket — Moving to the *basket* quickly while in *possession* of the ball.

drop step — When a player on *offense* goes to the *post position* and faces away from the *basket*. He then takes the ball. He moves next to a defender by taking a step backward and turns and goes toward the basket to make a *shot*.

dunk, dunk shot — Powerfully *jamming* the ball in the *basket* after leaping up toward the *rim*. See *stuff* and *stuff shot*.

A player gets ready to dunk.

E

elbowing — A *personal foul* happens when someone pushes his elbow into an opponent.

elimination tournament — If a team loses one game, it is out of an elimination tournament.

end line — This marks the end of each side of the *court*. This is a place where *shooters* try to make a *shot* right inside the line. See *baseline*.

established position — When a player on *defense* sets himself with his feet on the floor. If a player on *offense* bumps into the defender, that is called *charging*.

exhibition game — This pits two pro teams against one another in the preseason. The game result doesn't count in the standings.

explosive — When a team starts to score *points* after a slow start and looks strong on *offense*.

F

fadeaway, fadeaway jumper, fallaway, fallaway jumper — A *shot* where the athlete moves away from the *basket* as he shoots.

fake, feint — Making it look like you will move one way and going another. This gets the opponent to move in the opposite direction.

false double foul — When the other team has two players cause *fouls*. The second *foul* takes place before review of the first *foul*. This results in a *foul* for each *penalty*.

false multiple foul — Fouling one opponent two times in a row. The player who was fouled gets a *free throw* for each *foul* against him.

fast break — On *offense*, to bring the ball down the *court* quickly to stop the *defense* from setting up well.

favorite — A team with a good chance of winning against a competitor.

feed — When a player on *offense* gets the ball to a teammate close to the *basket*, so that player can score.

field goal — Two *points* given to the *offense* if the ball goes through the *basket*. In pro play, if the ball goes in the *basket* from 22 feet or more, the *offense* gets three *points*.

fill the lane — On *offense*, when players run down the *sidelines* toward the *basket*. This makes it harder for the *defense* to *cover* them because on offense the players are all over the *court*.

Final Four — West, East, Midwest, and Southeast college *basketball* teams meet during the 64-team *NCAA Tournament*. Winners move ahead and are then narrowed to four teams, with one named the national *NCAA* champion after a final game.

finals — In a tournament, these games decide the overall winner.

finals, NBA — One post-season game featuring the two best *NBA* teams playing each other.

finger roll — Using the fingers to roll the ball in the *basket* from close range.

first-string, first team — Those athletes who play first and play well.

five — The number of players on the *court* from one team during a game, practice, or scrimmage.

five-second rule — In college ball, a player with the ball on *offense* must *shoot* or *pass* the ball within five seconds if a defender is within six feet of him. If this doesn't occur, the other team is awarded a *throw-in* from *out-of-bounds* near the *violation*.

flagrant foul — A *foul* resulting in the doer's ejection from the game and a *personal* and *team foul*. This results in two *free throws* for the *offense*. This also means when a player tries to injure an opponent on purpose by kicking him or running into him while the player is in the air.

flip — Requires a fast snap of the wrist to get the ball to a player.

flip pass — An underhand *pass* using a snap of the wrists to get the ball to a teammate.

flood — When several teammates go to a part of the *court* to crush the opposition's *defense*.

floor — Where players play *basketball*.

floor violation — When a player breaks the game rules, but the *violation* is not serious enough that he harms a rival or blocks his movement. In this case, the other team gets the ball.

force — A *pass* thrown to a teammate whom the *defense* has covered.

forecourt — Located in the *frontcourt*, between the *end line* and the *midcourt markers*.

forfeit — When a team loses a game because it didn't follow the rules.

forward — Two taller players who play on *offense*, one on each side of the *basket*. They are good *rebounders* and *shooters*.

forwards — These two teammates play on opposite sides of the *court* near the *pivot* and the *basket* in the *frontcourt*.

A forward tries to get rebounds.

foul — Breaking game rules by showing *unsportsmanlike conduct*, making incorrect physical contact, or going against game regulations. The player who does the illegal action gets a foul and sometimes the team gets a foul.

foul lane — A rectangular space in between the *free-throw line* and the *end line*. When on *offense*, players may not stay in this area for more than three seconds in a row. During a *free throw*, players can't go in this area until the ball reaches the *rim, backboard,* or *net*. See *free-throw lane*.

foul line — The line from where players take *free-throw shots*. This line is parallel to the court's *end line*. See *free-throw line*.

foul out — When a player has a certain number of *fouls* called against him by the *officials*, he must leave the game and sit on his team's *bench*.

foul shot — When a player takes a *shot* from the *foul line*.

four-corner offense — This *offense* plans to take time off the *clock* by having players hold the ball and not letting the other team have it. It also makes the *defense* work hard because each player on *offense* plays at one corner of the *frontcourt*. The free teammate on *offense* stays in the *center-circle* area. The teammates then *pass* the ball to each other.

four-point play — When a player makes four *points* for his team because, even though he was fouled in three-point range, he makes the *basket* from three-point range. He is given a *free throw*, and by making it, he scores one extra *point* for a total of four *points*.

free — A player on *offense* not *covered* by an opponent.

free agent, restricted — When a pro player's contract ends, his team may offer him more money. This is to keep him from leaving for another team that wants him.

free agent, unrestricted — When a pro player's contract ends or a team *waives* him, he may go to another team for the same or more money. Pro players may choose this if they have at least five years in the *NBA* and two completed contracts.

free ball — A ball that either team can get. No one has *possession* of it while it's in the air or rolling on the court. See *loose ball*.

free throw — A *shot* given to a player or team because of a *foul*. The *shot* takes place from the *free-throw line*, where no one can *block* it.

free-throw area — The *free-throw lane* and the *free-throw circle*.

free-throw circle — Found at the top of the *key*, these circles are cut into by the *free-throw lines*. Sometimes, *jump balls* take place here.

free-throw lane — A rectangular space in between the *free-throw line* and the *end line*. When on *offense*, players may not stay in this area for more than three seconds in a row. During a *free throw*, players can't go in this area until the ball reaches the *rim*, *backboard*, or *net*. See *foul lane*.

free-throw line — The line from where players take *free-throw shots*. This line is parallel to the *court's end line*. See *foul line*.

free-throw line extended — A pretend line that helps *officials* decide where on the *court throw-ins* will take place. The line runs from the *sideline* to the *free-throw line*.

freeze — Keeping *possession* of the ball and delaying with it to hold on in a close game. See *stall*.

from the floor — A number showing the percentage of *shots* a player makes from all places on the *court* rather than the *free-throw line* only.

front — On *defense*, when a player gets between his rival and the ball to keep the rival from passing or scoring.

frontcourt — Part of the *basketball court* that has the *basket* that a team *shoots* at rather than defends. This also means the position of the *center* and the two *forwards* on a squad. See *front line*.

front lay-in, front lay-up — *Lay-ups* made by going to the front of the *basket* rather than the side.

front line — This part of the *basketball court* has the *basket* that a team *shoots* at rather than defends. This also means the position of the *center* and the two *forwards* on a squad. See *frontcourt*.

full-court press — When a team on *defense guards* the other squad man-to-man for the entire *court*. This *defense* forces the other team to play without mistakes on *offense* or risk turning over the ball.

This player's team is using a full-court press.

G

game clock — A *clock* that keeps track of the time left for the players to play during a *period*.

game plan — How a squad plans to win a game. This includes the *lineup* and offensive and defensive ideas that it will use to beat the other team.

give-and-go — When a player passes the ball to a teammate and then races past the opponent to an open space. He then catches the ball as it's thrown from his teammate.

Globetrotters — A team of black players that entertains people by using great *basketball* skills and funny routines. It travels the world to amuse fans. See *Harlem Globetrotters*.

goal — The *backboard, rim,* and *net* of a *basketball hoop*. This also means when a team makes a *basket* by shooting from the field or making a *free throw*.

goal game — When the game's purpose is to get the ball into the *net*.

goaltending — A *penalty* against a team for trying to stop a *shot* by touching it as it is about to go over the *rim*, or while the ball goes downward toward the *basket* before it hits the *rim*, or trying to touch it after it hits the *backboard*. For those who cause the *penalty*, the other team gets to throw the ball in from the *free-throw area*, or the *offense* gets two *points*—three *points* for the pros and some college teams if the shooter was in the three-point range when the *penalty* happened. See *basket interference*.

go backdoor — To try a *backdoor play* to make a lay-up underneath the basket.

go baseline — To play near the *baseline* to get a *pass* close in to the *basket*.

guard — Covering a rival so he can't make a *basket, dribble,* catch a *pass,* or throw a *pass* to a teammate.

guarding — Staying near a player to keep him from passing, shooting, or going toward the *basket.*

guards — Two players who work to bring the ball down the *court,* run the *offense,* and *pass* the ball to teammates who are in place to *shoot.* These players are good *ball handlers* and can be counted on to *shoot* well, too.

gunner — Someone who tries to make a *basket* all the time rather than passing to a teammate who is in a better position to score.

gunning — Someone who takes many *shots* at the *basket,* even when his teammates may be in a better place to make *baskets.*

This player is guarding a rival.

H

hack — This ends in a *personal foul* when a player chops at a rival's arm with his hand or arm to get the ball.

hacking — This ends in a *personal foul* when a player chops at an opponent's arm.

half — In the pros, a game has two *periods* in the first half of the game and two *periods* in the second half.

half-court press — When a team on *defense guards* the other squad man-to-man in the *backcourt*.

halftime — When the players take a break to get instruction from the *coach*.

Hall of Fame — Located in Springfield, Massachusetts, this museum features the finest *basketball* players. Named the Naismith Memorial Basketball Hall of Fame, it honors basketball's founder, Dr. James Naismith. See *Basketball Hall of Fame*.

hammer the boards — A player who moves with power to get near the *backboard* to grab *rebounds*. See *bang the boards, bang the glass, crash the boards, pound the boards,* and *pound the glass*.

hand check — This ends in a *personal foul* when a player on *defense* uses his hand and keeps touching his rival.

Harlem Globetrotters — A team of black players that entertains people by using great *basketball* skills and funny routines. It travels worldwide to amuse fans. See *Globetrotters*.

hashmark — A short line that begins at the side boundary line and runs parallel to the *end line*. See *midcourt area marker*.

held ball—When two opponents go after the ball and both grab the ball tightly, but no one person can say he had the ball first. A *jump ball* takes place at the *circle* closest to where this scrambling happened.

high percentage shot—A *shot* with a good chance of going in the *basket*.

high post—On *offense*, the *center* will most likely be here in the *frontcourt*. He will be positioned outside the *lane* next to the *free-throw line*. The *center*, from this spot, will *shoot*, *pass*, catch passes, and set *screens* for his offensive unit.

hold, holding—A forbidden action that results in a *penalty*. This happens when a player uses his hands to stop the rival from moving.

home court advantage—Playing at a team's own *court*, where the fans cheer for them.

home stand—Several games played in a row at a team's home *court*.

hook—A player on *offense* places himself sideways when facing the basket. Trying to make a *shot*, he lifts the ball over his head with one hand and flicks it with his wrist. This also means a player on *offense* makes a *personal foul* by having his back to a defender and then using an arm or a hand to hold that defender as he moves around the defender and to the *basket*. See *hook shot*.

hook pass—Placing himself sideways when facing the *basket*, the player on *offense* lifts the ball over his head with one hand and flicks it to a teammate for a *pass*.

hook shot—A player on *offense* places himself sideways when facing the *basket*. Trying to make a *shot*, he lifts the ball over his head with one hand and flicks it with his wrist. This also means a player on *offense* makes a *personal foul* by having his back to a defender and then using an arm or a hand to hold that defender as he moves around the defender and to the *basket*. See *hook*.

hoop — The *basket*.

H.O.R.S.E. — A game where people try to match competitors' shots. The first person shoots at the *basket*, and if he makes the *shot*, the next person and all playing must *shoot* from the same spot. If the people following the *shooter* don't make the *shot*, they collect the letter "H." The object is to collect the fewest letters in the word "horse."

hot dog — A player who shows off.

hot hand — A period when someone *shoots* the ball well.

Every player wants to get the ball in the hoop to score a basket.

I

inbound — A team has five seconds to throw the ball from the *sideline* into the *court* for play. If it doesn't, it turns the ball over to the other team for a *throw-in*.

inbound pass — When a team throws the ball from the *sideline* into the *court* for play.

in bounds, inbounds — A ball on the *basketball court* and in the area of play. This also means getting the ball in play with a player tossing it in from the *court's sideline*.

incidental contact — Bodily contact against a rival that is allowed on *offense* and *defense*.

inside — The area on the *court* close to the *basket* and near the *free-throw lane*.

inside game — A team or a person's ability to *shoot*, move, and *rebound* well close to the *basket*.

inside shooting — Known as *shots* at the *basket* from close range.

intentional foul — When a team is losing and it *fouls* a player on purpose while on *defense*. It does this to get the ball, so that it may make some *baskets* on *offense*.

intercept — Catching a ball meant for someone else.

in the paint — The *foul lane*, which is painted differently from the rest of the court.

isolate a defender — On *offense*, moving one player on *defense* into a setting where he plays *one-on-one* with a rival.

J

jab step — Trying to trick a rival on *defense* by *faking* a *drive* one way with a quick step, then going the other way to *pass*, *shoot* a *basket*, or go down the *court*.

jam — To *stuff* the ball in the *basket*.

jump ball — The *official* will toss the ball in the air between two rivals from a *restraining circle* on the *court* to start the game, in *overtime* play, or during the game. The two players try to *tap* the ball to a teammate, who will then take *possession*.

Going up for a jumper.

jumper — A type of *shot* known as a jump.

jumping circle — A player must have at least one foot in the center of this *restraining circle* when a *jump ball* starts the game, for a *jump ball* in *overtime* play, or for a *jump ball* during a game.

jump pass — Jumping while passing the ball.

jump shot — A player jumping and taking a *shot* at the *basket* with the ball over his head.

K

keepaway game — Keeping the ball from defenders with careful play and *ball control*. A plan usually used during a close game.

key, keyhole — The *free-throw lane* and the *free-throw area*.

kicking — An illegal play ending with a player moving the ball by using his foot, knee, or leg.

L

lane — The *free-throw lane* or the areas that players on *offense* use during a *fast break*, when these players run to each *sideline* to try to make it tough on the *defense* by spreading out.

lay-up, lay-in — When a player moves toward the *basket*, leaps, and tosses the ball against the *backboard* for a *basket*.

lead — Having more *points* than the other team.

leading the receiver — To *pass* the ball to a spot ahead of the *receiver*, so that he runs to get it.

lead official, leading official — This *official* heads down the *court* on each play before the players. He watches action near the *basket* and off the *court*.

league — Teams that play each other during a season.

line — The *free-throw line*.

lineup — The people on the *court* playing for one team.

live ball — A ball on the *court* and in play.

loose ball — A ball that either team can get. No one has *possession* of it while it's in the air or rolling on the court. See *free ball*.

loose-ball foul — At the pro level, this is a *personal foul* happening when no one has *possession* of the ball because it's in the air or rolling on the court. *Fouls* go against the team and the responsible player. The other team gets to throw the ball in from the *sidelines* at the penalty spot.

lowbridge — A *personal foul* and the fouled player gets two *free throws*. The *foul* happens when someone runs into a player's legs while he is in the air shooting or making a play on *offense*. See *submarine* and *undercut*.

lower percentage shot—A *shot* unlikely to go in the *basket*.

low post—On *offense*, the *center* will most likely be here in the *frontcourt*, located outside the *free-throw lane* near the basket. The *center*, from this spot, will *shoot, pass,* catch passes, and set *screens* for his offensive unit.

No player wants to take a lower percentage shot.

M

man-on-man defense, man-to-man defense — When one player *guards* an assigned opponent.

March Madness — The *NCAA Tournament* that decides a college national champion. The tournament begins in March.

match — Two teams playing each other.

match-ups — Two players on different teams who play against each other on *offense* and *defense*.

midcourt — The *frontcourt* between the *center line* and the *hashmarks*.

midcourt area marker — A short line that begins at the side boundary line and runs parallel to the *end line*. See *hashmark*.

midcourt line — This line divides the *court* into the *backcourt* and *frontcourt*. It runs parallel to the *end lines*. See *center line* and *division line*.

middle — Indicates the space near the *free-throw line*.

mismatch — When a small opponent covers a tall player.

moving pick — When a player on *offense* doesn't stay put while trying to *block* the path of a defensive player. A *personal foul* happens if the player on *offense* runs into the player on *defense*.

multiple foul — When two or more teammates *foul* one player at the same time. The result is a *free throw* given to the fouled player for each *foul* made against him.

MVP — This means most valuable player. Given to the best player, who helped his team the most during regular-season or tournament play.

N

NBA — National Basketball Association.

NCAA — The National Collegiate Athletic Association, a group that helps college students who are athletes.

NCAA Tournament — A contest among 68 teams picked to play in the tournament to decide a college *basketball* champion.

net — The white material attached to the basket where the players want the ball to go in and through. See *cord*.

Try to shoot the ball in the net.

NIT — National Invitation Tournament. A contest with 32 college *basketball* teams that do not play in the *NCAA Tournament*.

no harm, no foul — Said of *officials* who will let play go on, even if a *foul* happens, if that *foul* didn't help the other team.

O

offense — Trying to make *baskets* while the other team tries to stop you from scoring.

offensive boards — The offense's *backboard* where they *shoot* to make *baskets*.

offensive foul — A *foul* against the team with *possession* of the ball.

offensive rebound — Grabbing the *rebound* from the *backboard* where a team *shoots* to score *points*.

official — Three *referees* who make sure games are played fairly and game time and *points* scored are correct.

off-season — When *basketball* players rest and have no planned games or practices.

off the dribble — Trying to make a *basket* while *dribbling* quickly toward it.

one-and-one — An extra *free throw* given to the fouled player if he makes the first *free throw* during *bonus* play. A *bonus* is given if the other team makes a certain amount of *fouls* during a certain time period. This rule applies to college ball. See *one-plus-one*.

one-handed push — A *shot* taken by placing a hand on the side of the ball to steady it, using the other hand to push the ball toward the *basket*. The fingers push the ball upward. See *one-hand set*.

one-hand set — A *shot* taken by placing a hand on the side of the ball to steady it, using the other hand to push the ball toward the *basket*. The fingers push the ball upward. *See one-handed push*.

one-on-one — When one player on a team plays against an opponent. He tries to play better than him on *offense* or *guard* him on *defense*.

one-plus-one — An extra *free throw* given to the fouled player if he makes the first *free throw* during *bonus* play. A *bonus* is given if the other team makes a certain amount of *fouls* during a certain time period. This rule applies to college ball. See *one-and-one*.

open — A player who has no rival near him, so he shoots or gets to the *basket* easier than a *covered* player.

OT, overtime — When a team *ties* at the end of regulation play, they play for five more minutes until one team *leads*. If after five minutes, they are *tied*, they keep on with overtime periods to decide a winner.

outlet — After a defensive *rebound*, this play includes passing to a player going up the *court* for a *fast break*.

outlet pass — After a defensive *rebound*, a player gets the ball and throws it *downcourt* to a teammate going there for a *fast break*.

out of bounds — Any area outside the *court's* boundaries. When a player or ball passes the boundaries, they are out of play. The ball then goes to the opposition for a *throw-in* from where the ball went out.

out-of-bounds play — When the *offense* has a *frontcourt throw-in*, it may use a special play where teammates run to different spots to catch a *pass*.

outrebound — When each team wants to get more *rebounds* than the other squad.

outshoot — The team that makes more *baskets* and takes more *shots* during a game.

outside — The part of the *frontcourt* that is near the *sidelines* and *division line* and far from the *basket*.

outside shooter — A player able to score a distance from the *basket* and shoot well.

outside shooting — *Shots* taken behind the foul circle from three-point range.

over and back — To avoid this *penalty*, players on *offense* must bring the ball over the *center line* within 10 seconds in college ball and eight seconds in pro ball. If they don't, they turn the ball over from the *sideline* at the point where the play stopped. Once a team goes past the *center line*, it must not throw or *dribble* the ball into the *backcourt*. If it does, it must give the ball to the other team to do a *throw-in*. This takes place from the *sideline* at the *center line*. See *backcourt violation*.

overhead pass — A good *pass* to throw the ball high, so the *defense* can't get it. To do this, the player holds the ball over his head with both hands. He quickly lets go of it by whipping his hands forward.

Getting ready for an overhead pass.

overload the zone — On *offense*, *flooding* an area with players to crush the *defense*.

overplay — Making the other team's *offense* play to its weakest side by putting lots of defenders on its strongest side.

over the limit — When a team makes more than seven *fouls* in a *half* during a college game or more than five *fouls* in a *quarter* in a pro game.

over the top — When a rival gets set in *position*, another player can't jump on him or put their body over him to make contact. If a player does make contact, he gets a *personal foul*. This also means a *basket* made from the *outside*, over the heads and arms of defenders.

P

paint — The area of the *free-throw lane*.

palm the ball — Breaking a rule when a player wrongly cups the ball in his hand, lifting it off the floor while he *dribbles*. The other team gets *possession* through a *sideline throw-in*.

pass — Throwing the ball to a teammate to allow him to score, or passing the ball to a teammate who's *open* or closer to the *basket*.

passer — A player who tosses the ball to a teammate.

passing lane — Finding an opening to get a *pass* to a teammate.

penalty — A rule infraction called by *officials* against a team or player. The other team gets *possession* of the ball or a player can shoot *foul shots* because of the *foul*.

penalty situation — In the pro game, when a squad has five *team fouls* per *period*, the other team gets two *free throws* for every following *foul*. See *penalty stage*.

penalty stage — In the pro game, when a squad has five *team fouls* per *period*, the other team gets two *free throws* for every following *foul*. See *penalty situation*.

perimeter — Distant *shots* at the *basket* behind the foul circle and from three-point range.

period — This is also known as a *quarter*. In the pros, four of these equal time frames amount to the time in one *basketball* game.

personal foul — Banned physical contact against the other team by *pushing, holding, charging, blocking, hacking,* or *elbowing*. If the *offense* makes these fouls, the other team gets a *throw-in* from the point of the infraction. The player on *offense* and the team each receive a *foul*.

Free throws take place if the *foul* is during or results in a *bonus situation* for the pro and college game.

A player who tries to *shoot* from two-point range, who is fouled during the process, receives two *free throws* if they didn't make the *shot*. A *shooter* who scores during the *foul* gets one *free throw*.

pick — On *offense*, a player gets in a set position beside, in front of, or behind a defensive rival. He does this to make it hard for that defender to get to the person on *offense* with the ball. To make this a good plan and not a *foul*, the offensive player cannot move until his teammate with the ball passes him in his set position. See *screen* or *screener*.

pick-and-roll — On *offense* a player gets in a set position beside, in front of, or behind a defensive rival. He wants to make it hard for that defender to get to the person on *offense* with the ball. The person on *offense* then leaves his position, goes to the *basket*, and gets ready for a teammate's *pass*.

picked off — When a defensive player can't reach the *ball handler* on *offense* because of a good offensive *screen*.

pickup games — A game not planned and played with any players.

pivot — The person told to play the *post* or pivot position. This also means the movement by a player with the ball. When he stops, he must keep one foot planted on the floor while he moves the other foot and his body in a circle to look for a teammate to whom he can throw the ball.

pivot foot — The foot planted on the floor by a player with the ball. When he stops, he must keep one foot planted on the floor while he moves the other foot and his body in a circle. The *penalty* for moving the planted foot is *traveling*. Then, the other team gets a *throw-in* from *out of bounds* near the point of the infraction.

pivotman — The person assigned to play the *post* or *pivot* position.

play-by-play — Telling what's happening in the game during a radio or TV show.

player control foul — When a player who has the ball makes a *foul*. This rule applies to college play. As a result of the *foul*, the team and the player have a *personal foul* counted against them. The other team then does a *throw-in* from *out of bounds* near the point of the *foul*.

play for one — A plan used toward the end of the game or a *period*. The team on *offense* holds the ball and keeps *possession*. It tries to keep the ball from the opponent who cannot take a final *shot*.

playmaker — An on-court player who tells the team how to run plays.

playmaking — Takes place on *offense* when a team runs some plays it practiced and throws the ball to teammates to make a *basket*.

point — How a team scores in *basketball*. A *field goal* is worth two points, a *free throw* is one point, and a *basket* made from the three-point area is three points. This also means, when on *offense*, the area where the *point guard* plays, in the back of the *frontcourt*.

point guard — A playmaker who is a good *dribbler* and *ball handler*. Because of his skills, he sets up offensive plays, brings the ball to the *frontcourt*, and often stays in the back area of the *frontcourt* when on *offense*.

Point guards are good dribblers.

position—When a defender sets his feet on the ground to *guard* a player on *offense*. If the defender is set before the person on *offense* gets to the defender's space, and if the player on *offense* runs into the defender, it's known as *charging*. This is illegal.

possession—When a team or person holds, *dribbles*, or passes the ball.

possession arrow—College officials use this to note the team allowed to *throw-in* the ball from the *sidelines* when starting a new *half* or tossing up a *jump ball*.

post—On *offense*, the *center* will most likely stand here in the *frontcourt*, located outside the *free-throw lane* near the *basket* or outside the *lane* next to the *free-throw line*. The *center*, from these spots, will *shoot*, *pass*, catch passes, and set *screens* for his offensive unit. The *low post* is near the *basket* and the *high post* is near the *free-throw lane*.

post man—He plays the *post position* for a team.

post position—When a player plays the *high-post* or *low-post* position.

post-up—A player who takes the *post position* near the *basket*.

pound the boards, pound the glass—A player who moves with power to get near the *backboard* to grab *rebounds*. See *bang the boards, bang the glass, crash the boards,* and *hammer the boards*.

power forward—A powerful player and tall man. His job is to get *rebounds* on *offense* and stop the *offense* from getting close to the *basket* and scoring.

press—On *defense*, when a team *guards* the other squad man-to-man in the *backcourt* or when the *defense guards* the rivals man-to-man from one end of the *court* to the other.

This *defense* allows a team to make another team play without mistakes on *offense* or chance turning over the ball.

protect a lead — Playing with control toward the end of the game to avoid giving the ball to the other team. This stops the other team from scoring, taking the *lead*, or having a *tie* game.

pump — Pretending to *shoot* a *basket* to fake out the defender and then passing, shooting, or *dribbling* the ball to another area.

pure shooter — A player skilled at shooting *baskets*.

pushing — When a player moves an opponent. Known as an illegal act and results in a *foul*.

push shot — A *shot* that doesn't use the wrists, but uses the fingertips to lift the ball and move it forward.

put the ball on the floor — When a player *dribbles* the ball.

Q

quadruple double — A player scoring double-digits in *points, rebounds, assists,* and *blocks* or *steals* during one game.

quarter — A specified amount of game time. In the pro game, a quarter lasts 12 minutes. There are four quarters, or *periods,* in a game.

quarterfinals — When playing in an *elimination tournament,* this game happens before the *semifinal* game.

Scoring a quadruple double is hard.

R

read — Deciding what a player might do on *offense* or *defense* and then acting quickly to get into position.

rebound — Getting the ball and keeping it once it hits the *backboard* or the *basket's rim*.

rebounder — Getting *rebounds* a lot.

receiver — Someone who catches a *pass*.

recover — Getting a *loose ball* under control.

ref — The *referee*.

referee — A person in charge of the game's rules and regulations. Three are on the *court* at one time.

regulation game — A game with no *overtime* play that lasts 48 minutes in the pro ranks and 40 minutes in college.

reject — When the *defense* reaches up and knocks down a *shot* at the *basket* by the *offense*.

release — To do different defensive actions on the *court* and then switch. For instance, *double-teaming* one player and then playing *man-to-man defense* on another player.

release early — On *offense*, to leave the *backcourt* early to start a *fast break*.

restraining circle — This is used for *jump-ball* action. There are three on the *court* — one in the center and one on each side of the *court*.

reverse dunk — When the player *stuffs* the ball in the *basket* while facing away from the *basket*.

reverse lay-in or reverse lay-up — When a player is close to the *basket* and he puts the ball under the rim and shoots it into the *basket* from the other side of the rim.

ride the bench — A *substitute* on a team and not a starting player.

rim — Round, with a *net* attached, and connected to each *backboard*.

rim shot — A ball that hits the *basket's rim*.

The ball is on the basket's rim.

rocker step — Done on *offense*, this has a player take a step then move backward to *shoot*.

roll — Moving from a stopped place and heading toward the *basket*.

rookie — An athlete playing his first year.

roster — The people who make up a team.

run — Quickly scoring a lot of *baskets* while the other team makes few *points*.

run and gun — A plan on *offense* using the *fast-break* play and steady shooting at the *basket*. See *run and shoot*.

run and shoot — A plan on *offense* using the *fast-break* play and steady shooting at the *basket*. See *run and gun*.

run the break — A player on *offense* helpful in getting the *fast-break* plan going well.

S

sag, sagging — When a player moves to the *basket* on *defense* to cover a player there instead of *guarding* a player farther away. This is also known as a collapsing defense.

scoop, scoop lay-up — On *offense*, when a player takes the ball in for a *lay-up*. He brings the ball up to the *backboard* underhand.

scorer — A person who tracks the *free throws* and *field goals* made, the *fouls* caused, and the *timeouts* taken by each team.

scoring opportunity — A player on *offense* able to score when free from defenders.

screen, screener — On *offense*, a player gets in a set position beside, in front of, or behind a defensive rival. He does this to make it hard for that defender to get to the person on *offense* with the ball. To make this a good plan and not a *foul*, the offensive player cannot move until his teammate with the ball passes him in his set position. See *pick*.

screen out — When a player gets in front of the opponent and tries to get the *rebound* or *tip-in* first. See *block out* and *boxing out*.

screen play — When a player on *offense* gets ready to *shoot* at the *basket* as his teammate blocks a defensive player on the other team.

seam — In a *zone defense*, this is an open space between two coverage zones.

second-string player — One who doesn't start a game.

semifinal — A game before the final game in an *elimination tournament*.

set a pick — Keeping a defensive player away with a *screen*.

set offense — An offense trying to get a *high percentage shot* at the *basket* by having teammates move into place to make that *shot*.

set play — On *offense*, a team seeks a *high percentage shot* at the *basket* by running this play. It has teammates move into place to make that *shot*.

set shot — A player on *offense* tries this *shot* with his feet on the ground.

shift — On *defense*, moving from covering one man to covering a different man because he is *open* or likely to score.

shoot — Trying to make a *basket*.

shootaround — Practicing *shots*, skills, and exercising during a short practice planned when games are close.

shooter — A player aiming at the *basket* and taking a *shot* to make *points*. This also means someone who can make *baskets*.

shooting clock — In pro ball, teams watch this *clock* to see how much time remains, according to the *24-second rule*. See *shot clock*.

shooting guard — A good *shooter* from a distance who serves as a backup *ball handler* to the *point guard*. These players are fast, can *dribble* well, and can find an opening to *shoot* or *pass* the ball to a teammate.

shooting range — The distance from the *basket* where a player can easily make a *field goal*.

shoot over the zone — When a team on *offense* always makes *shots* from farther away, it makes the defense switch from its *zone defense* to a man-to-man plan.

shot — Tossing the ball up at the *basket* to try and make a *field goal*.

shot clock — Pro teams watch this *clock* to see how much time remains to *shoot*, according to the *24-second rule*. See *shooting clock*.

shot clocker — A *clock* that guides players. It lets them know they need to *shoot* the ball before time passes on a *24-second* or *35-second clock*. If not, an infraction takes place.

shotmaker — A good *shooter*.

shovel pass — Using an underhand motion to make a *pass* to a teammate.

sidelines — The space outside the lines of the *court* where the players sit when out of the game.

sink — When the *basketball* goes in the *hoop*.

sixth man — When a player needs a rest, or someone needs to sit on the bench because of *foul* trouble or poor play, this man comes in often as a *substitute* for the player who left the game.

sky — Going upward easily.

skyhook — When someone takes a *hook shot* above the *basket's rim*.

slam dunk — *Jamming* the ball into the *basket* harder than in a *dunk*.

small forward — A smaller player placed at *forward* who is good at shooting and who moves with speed and agility.

spot pass — A *pass* ahead of a player who moves to that *pass* and gets it while on the run.

spread-court offense, spread offense — A plan where the *offense* passes the ball and keeps play to the outside of the *frontcourt*. By doing so, the *offense* hopes to have the *defense* switch from *zone defense* to man-to-man, using the middle of the *court* to score.

squaring up — Facing frontward toward the *basket* when shooting.

stack — Using the *forwards* on *offense* to play *low-post* positions on each side of the *lane*. This sometimes causes the *center* to play a *low-post* position on the other side of the *lane*.

stall — Keeping *possession* of the ball and delaying with it to hold on in a close game. See *freeze*.

stall ball—To keep the ball on *offense* with good passing and *dribbling*. By using this plan, the rival might make defensive mistakes or play in a different way.

starting lineup—Five teammates who begin the game and usually have the squad's best *basketball* skill set.

Each team has a starting lineup.

steal—Taking the ball from an opponent while he's *dribbling*, or catching a *pass* meant for the other team.

steps—An illegal play where a person with the ball holds the ball and walks with it or moves the *pivot foot* when he has the ball. The other team gets to *throw-in* the ball from the sideline near the point of the infraction.

strong side—The side of the *court* where the ball is in play.

stuff—Powerfully *jamming* the ball in the *basket* after leaping up toward the *rim*. See *dunk, dunk shot,* and *stuff shot*.

stuff shot—Powerfully *jamming* the ball in the *basket* after leaping up toward the *rim*. See *dunk, dunk shot,* and *stuff*.

stutter step — Changing movement or direction to throw off a defender and get by him.

submarine — A *personal foul* and the fouled player gets two *free throws*. The *foul* happens when someone runs into a player's legs while he is in the air shooting or making a play on *offense*. See *lowbridge* and *undercut*.

substitute — An athlete who enters the game to replace a hurt or tired player.

swing — Able to play two positions on a team — usually *forward* and *guard*.

swingman — An athlete who plays two positions on a team.

swish — When the *basketball* enters the *basket* and doesn't touch the *rim* or *backboard*.

switch — *Guarding* someone on *offense* who isn't covered or changing defensive tasks with a teammate.

T

T — A *technical foul*.

tap — The *tipoff*, a *jump ball* between players. See *tip*.

tap-in — A player makes two *points* by using the fingertips to push the ball into the *basket* after a *rebound*.

team foul — A team can have a certain number of *fouls* during a time frame before the *bonus* or *penalty situation* begins. A team foul counts toward those *fouls*.

technical foul — The most serious of *fouls* that includes *unsportsmanlike conduct*, contact on purpose, or obvious bad behavior against an opponent. In college, the opposition gets two *free throws* and the ball goes to the team that had the ball at the time of the infraction for a *throw-in* from *out of bounds*.

ten-second line — In college ball, the *offense* must bring the ball over this line, known as the *division line*, within 10 seconds of taking *possession* of the ball in the *backcourt*.

ten-second rule — Once the *offense* gets the ball in its *backcourt*, it has 10 seconds to bring the ball to the *frontcourt* in college ball.

thirty-five second clock — In college ball, the *offense* keeps an eye on this *clock*. The offense has 35 seconds to *shoot* the *basketball*. If it doesn't, it must give the ball to the other team.

thirty-five second rule — In college ball, the *offense* has 35 seconds to *shoot* at the *basket* after taking *possession* of the ball.

thirty-five second violation — Happens when a college team does not *shoot* the ball within 35 seconds of *possession*.

thread the needle — Throwing the ball well to a teammate located between defenders.

three-point field goal — When the *offense* makes a *basket* from three-point range, about 23 feet from the *basket* in pro ball. The distance is 20 feet, nine inches from the *basket* in college ball.

three-point line — A line that marks the area where a *basket* counts for three *points*, about 23 feet from the *basket* in pro ball. The line is in the shape of an arc coming out from each *baseline*. In college ball, the line is 20 feet, nine inches from the *basket*.

three-point play — If a player tries to *shoot*, makes the *basket*, and he's fouled, that player gets one *free throw*. That brings the play's total *points* to three if he makes the *basket* from the *foul line*.

three-point shot — Three points *awarded a shooter* for a *basket* made behind the *three-point line*.

Taking a three-point shot requires skill.

three-second area, three-second lane — When the *three-second rule* is in place, this is the *free-throw lane*.

three-second rule — On *offense*, no player can stay in the *free-throw lane* for more than three seconds.

three-second violation—A player on *offense* in the *free-throw lane* for more than three seconds. For that infraction, the other team gets the ball for a *throw-in* from *out of bounds*.

thrower-in—The person in charge of throwing the ball in from the *sidelines*.

throw-in—A team has five seconds to get the ball in play from *out of bounds* after a rules infraction, a basket, or a ball out of play. If the ball doesn't get in play within five seconds, the ball goes to the other team for a throw-in from the same spot.

ticky-tack foul—A *foul* called without cause because it did not affect play.

tie—If two teams have the same *point* total at the end of the game, the contest goes into *overtime* play. The team with the higher score at the end of *overtime* wins.

tie ball—When two rivals go after the ball, both grab the ball tightly, but no one person can say they got the ball first.

timekeeper—Keeps time during a game.

time line—The *division line*, when used with the *ten-second rule*, does not allow the team to have the ball for more than 10 seconds in its *backcourt*.

timeout—Each pro team gets seven of these in a *regulation game*. Play stops for a short time, with the *coach* talking to players about their role on the *court*.

timer—These people keep track of the length of the game, *timeouts*, and *periods*. There are two timers in a game.

tip—A *tipoff*, a *jump ball* between players. See *tap*.

tip-in — When a player gets near the *basket* and lightly taps in a *rebound, shot*, or *pass*.

tipoff — This starts the game or *period* and is a *jump ball* between two players.

top of the key — The area slightly inside and outside the *restraining circle* and behind the *free-throw line*.

toss-up — A *jump ball*.

traffic — A lot of players in the same area, usually defensive players.

trail official — This *official* looks to see if a *basket* went in and watches play from behind, near the middle of the *court*. He notes any rule infractions, along with the other *officials*.

transition — After a *basket*, a team goes on *offense*, beginning in its *backcourt*.

transition game — Able to go on *offense* after a *basket*, beginning in the *backcourt*.

trap — Quickly asking two men to *guard* one player. This also means having the ball pressed against the *backboard*.

travel — A *violation* where a player holds the ball rather than *dribbles* it or moves a *pivot foot*.

traveling — When a player holds the ball instead of *dribbling* it or moves a *pivot foot*. Then, the ball goes to the other team for a *throw-in* from the point of infraction. See *walking*.

triple doubles — When a player reaches double figures in three areas— *points* scored, *assists*, and *rebounds*.

triple-team — Asking three people to *cover* one player at the same time.

turnaround jumper — A *jump shot* made while turning around toward the *basket*.

turnaround jump shot — On *offense*, while facing the *backcourt*, a player spins toward the offensive *basket*. Then, he jumps in the air and *shoots* the ball at the *basket* while in the air.

turnover — When a team loses the ball to the competitors.

twenty-four-second clock — In pro *basketball*, a team has 24 seconds to take a *shot* at the *basket*. This *clock* keeps track of that time.

twenty-four-second rule — In pro *basketball*, a team has 24 seconds to take a *shot* at the *basket*.

twenty-four-second violation — When a pro team takes more than 24 seconds to *shoot* the ball at the *basket* it must give the ball to the other team for a *throw-in*.

two-handed push — Taking the ball over the head and using a snap of the wrists to get it to the *basket*.

two-hand set shot — When a player on *offense* shoots at the *basket* by taking the ball in two hands, placing it at neck level, and then using the fingertips to move the ball up with help from a push from the legs.

two-shot foul — When a person gets to *shoot* two *free throws* because of a *personal* or *technical foul*.

U

umpire — Often called a *referee*, he is one of three *officials* on the *court* who decides *fouls, penalties,* and *center jumps.*

undercut — A *personal foul* and the fouled player gets two *free throws.* The *foul* happens when someone runs into a player's legs while he is in the air shooting or making a play on *offense.* See *lowbridge* and *submarine.*

underneath — Close to or underneath the *basket.*

unmarked — A player on *offense, open* and unguarded.

unsportsmanlike conduct — A *coach* or player gets a *technical foul* or is removed from the game if he swears, hits another player or an *official,* or acts badly on the *court.*

upcourt — The area where a team *shoots* at the *basket.*

upset — When the underdog defeats the team picked to win.

utility — A good player able to play different positions on the *court* when a *first-string* player can't play.

Basketball umpire, or referee

V

violation — When the squad with the ball breaks the rules. Because of that, the other team gets to *throw-in* the ball.

W

walking — When a player holds the ball instead of *dribbling* it or moves a *pivot foot*. Then, the other team gets a *throw-in* from the point of infraction. See *traveling*.

weak side — The side of the *court* opposite the ball.

weave — When a team has its players move in a way that looks like a figure-eight while passing the ball to each other. The goal is to get close enough to *shoot* and make a *basket*.

wild-card team — A team moving to the playoffs because it had the best win-loss record among remaining teams. This team did not meet the requirements to go to the playoffs right away.

wing — A *forward* on *offense* who plays near the *baseline* or by either of the *lanes*.

This athlete plays wing.

Y

yo-yoing — Not moving with the ball, but bouncing it up and down in one place.

Z

zone—On *defense*, when a player *guards* a certain part of the *court*.

zone defense—A plan on *defense* where a player *guards* a certain part of the *court* instead of one rival.

zone press—Using *man-to-man defense* when a player on *offense* moves to a place where a defender is already using *zone defense*.

Teams use the zone defense to guard a certain part of the court instead of one player.

INDEX

A

All-America, 19
All-Star, 19

B

Backcourt violation, 20
Basket, 2, 21
Bobcats, Charlotte, 11
Bounce pass, 9, 23
Boxing out, 23
Box score, 23
Bucks, Milwaukee, 11
Bulls, Chicago, 11

C

Cavaliers, Cleveland, 11
Celtics, Boston, 11
Center, 2, 16, 25
Center circle, 25
Charging, 25
Chest pass, 9, 25
Clippers, Los Angeles, 12
Clock, game, 6, 39
Clock, shot, 6, 64
Conferences, NBA, 11
Court, 1, 13, 27
Crossover dribble, 27

D

Dead ball, 29
Defense, 8, 14, 29
Defensive rebound, 29
Diagram, basketball court, 13
Diagram, defense, 14
Diagram, offense, 14
Diagram, official's signals, 17

Double dribble, 30
Dribble, 9, 30
Dunk, 10, 31

E

Eastern Conference, 11
End line, 32
Established position, 32

F

Fast break, 8, 33
Field goal, 4, 33
Final Four, 33
Finals, NBA, 34
5-second rule, 34
Flagrant foul, 4, 34
Floor violation, 4, 34
Forward, 2, 35
Forward, power, 15
Forward, small, 15
Foul, 4, 35
Foul lane, 35
Foul line, 5, 35
Foul, personal, 4, 54
Foul, shot, 5, 36
Foul, team, 5, 68
Foul, technical, 4, 68
Free throw, 4, 36
Free-throw line, 5, 37
Full-court press, 38

G

Game clock, 6, 39
Grizzlies, Memphis, 12
Guard, 2, 40
Guard, point, 15
Guard, shooting, 15

H

Halftime, 6, 41
Hand signals, official's, 17
Hawks, Atlanta, 11
Heat, Miami, 11
Hook shot, 10, 42
Hornets, New Orleans, 12

I

Inbounds, 44

J

Jazz, Utah, 11
Jump ball, 7, 45
Jump pass, 45
Jump shot, 10, 45

K

Key, 46
Kings, Sacramento, 12
Knickerbockers, New York, 11

L

Lakers, Los Angeles, 12
Lay-up or lay-in, 47
Live ball, 47
Loose ball, 47

M

Magic, Orlando, 11
Man-to-man defense, 8, 49
March Madness, 49
Mavericks, Dallas, 12
Midcourt line, 1, 49
Most Valuable Player, 49

N

Naismith, James, 1
NBA, 50
NBA playoffs, 12
NBA teams, 11
NCAA, 50
Net, 2, 50
Nets, New Jersey, 11
NIT, 50
Nuggets, Denver, 11

O

Offense, 7, 14, 51
Offensive rebound, 51
Officials, 3, 51
Official's hand signals, 17
One-on-one, 51
One-plus-one or one-and-one, 5, 52
Outlet pass, 9, 52
Out of bounds, 52
Overhead pass, 9, 53
Overtime, 6

P

Pacers, Indiana, 11
Paint, in the, 54
Passes, types of, 9
Period, 54
Pick, 8, 55
Pistons, Detroit, 11
Point guard, 15, 56
Post, high, 57
Post, low, 57

Q

Quarter, 59

R

Raptors, Toronto, 11
Rebound, 4, 60
Referee, 3, 60
Rim, 2, 61
Rockets, Houston, 12

S

Screen, 63
Set shot, 10, 64
76ers, Philadelphia, 11
Shooting, 10
Shooting guard, 15, 64
Shot clock, 6, 64
Sidelines, 1, 65
Slam dunk, 65
Spurs, San Antonio, 12
Substitute, 3, 7, 67
Suns, Phoenix, 12

T

10-second rule, 6, 68
35-second clock, 6, 68
3-point line, 4, 69
3-point play, 69
3-point shot, 69
3-second violation, 70
Throw-in, 70
Thunder, Oklahoma City, 11
Timberwolves, Minnesota, 11
Timeout, 7, 70
Tipoff, 71
Trailblazers, Portland, 11
Traveling, 71
Turnover, 72
24-second clock, 6, 72
24-second violation, 6, 72

U

Umpire, 3, 73
Uniforms, 2

V

Violation, 74

W

Walking, 75
Warriors, Golden State, 12
Western Conference, 11
Wizards, Washington, 11

Z

Zone defense, 8, 77

CPSIA information can be obtained
at www.ICGtesting.com
Printed in the USA
FSOW01n2220131216
28561FS